All About Science

All About
Magnetism

Angela Royston

capstone®

© 2016 Heinemann-Raintree
an imprint of Capstone Global Library, LLC
Chicago, Illinois

To contact Capstone Global Library please call 800-747-4992, or visit our web site www.capstonepub.com

Edited by Linda Staniford
Designed by Steve Mead
Picture research by Kelly Garvin
Production by Victoria Fitzgerald
Originated by Capstone Global Library Ltd

Library of Congress Cataloging-in-Publication Data
Cataloging-in-publication information is on file with the Library of Congress.
Written by Angela Royston
ISBN 978-1-4846-2690-0 (hardcover)
ISBN 978-1-4846-2694-8 (paperback)
ISBN 978-1-4846-2698-6 (eBook PDF)

Acknowledgments
The author and publisher are grateful to the following for permission to reproduce copyright material:
Capstone Press/Karon Dubke, 4, 6, 7, 8, 12, 13, 14, 15, 16, 17, 18, 19, 20, 21, 26, 29; Corbis/Lance Iverson/San Francisco Chronicle, 11; Glow Images/Gavin Hellier/Robert Harding, 23; iStockphoto: colematt, 5; Science Source/Lawrence Lawry, cover; Shutterstock: AlexLMX, 24, dvande, 10, mamahoohooba, 22, Opka, 25, rayjunk, 27

We would like to thank Pat O'Mahony for his help in the preparation of this book.

Contents

Some words are shown in bold, **like this.** You can find out what they mean by looking in the glossary.

What Is Magnetism?

A magnet has a force that pulls certain objects toward it. For example, refrigerator and freezer doors have a rubber strip around the edge. This contains a magnet, which pulls the door tightly shut.

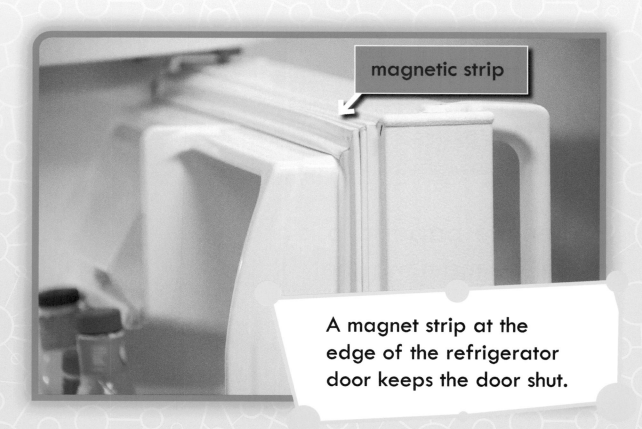

magnetic strip

A magnet strip at the edge of the refrigerator door keeps the door shut.

Magnetism works even when the magnet is not touching the object. If the magnet is close enough, it pulls the object toward it.

The magnet's magnetic force begins to lift the nails before the magnet touches them.

Shapes of Magnets

Most magnets are shaped like a bar or a horseshoe. The magnetic force is strongest at the ends of these magnets. Ring magnets are round with a hole in the middle, like a doughnut.

Big magnets are stronger than small magnets.

ring magnet

bar magnet

keeper

horseshoe magnet

This little plastic man has small magnets hidden inside his hands.

Milk
Bread

When a bar or horseshoe magnet is not being used, a metal bar is placed across the ends. The bar is called a **keeper,** and it stops the magnetic force from leaking away.

Magnetic or nonmagnetic?

Materials that are attracted to a magnet are called magnetic. Materials that are not attracted to a magnet are nonmagnetic. Test some objects for magnetism with this magnet test.

You will need:

✓ a magnet

✓ objects made of different materials, such as plastic blocks, a wooden toy, construction paper, a nail, and an empty soda can

1 Make a table like the one shown here.

2 Test each material with the magnet and fill in the table.

Material	Magnetic	Nonmagnetic
plastic blocks		
wooden toy		
construction paper		
nail		
empty soda can		

Check your results on page 28.

Using Magnets

Magnets are used in many different ways. Some toy trains use magnets to connect the cars. Cases for smartphones may use magnets to close them easily.

A very strong magnet lifts a heavy load of crushed scrap metal.

A magnet sorts nonmagnetic aluminum cans from steel cans.

Iron and steel are magnetic. All other materials and most other metals are nonmagnetic. This allows **recycling centers** to use magnets to separate iron and steel from other **scrap metal**.

Exploring Magnetic Force

When something magnetic is attached to a magnet, it becomes a temporary magnet. For example, a metal paper clip attached to a magnet becomes a temporary magnet. It can then **attract** another metal paper clip.

You need a strong magnet to make a long chain of steel paper clips.

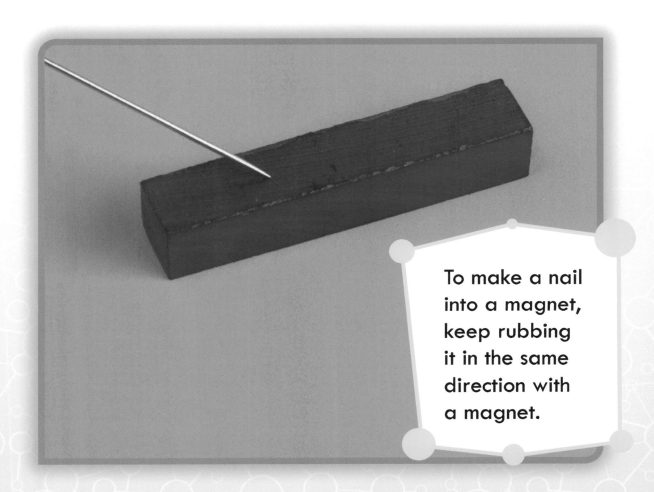

To make a nail into a magnet, keep rubbing it in the same direction with a magnet.

When the paper clip is separated from the main magnet, it stops being a temporary magnet. You can also make something magnetic, such as a paper clip or nail, into a magnet by rubbing it with a permanent magnet.

Which magnet is the strongest?

You will need:

✓ 3 or 4 magnets of different size and shape

✓ a nail

✓ a sheet of paper

✓ a ruler and pencil

1 Draw a line across the paper and place the nail on it as shown in the photo.

2 Slowly move the first magnet across the paper toward the line.

3 Mark the place where the magnet begins to move the nail.

4 Repeat with the other magnets. Which magnet is the strongest?

Check your results on page 28.

What Can Magnetic Force Pass Through?

A magnet can **attract** a magnetic object even when there is a gap between them. This means that magnetic force can pass through air. It can also pass through other materials, including paper, water, and glass.

Small magnets can hold a sheet of paper onto a metal door.

As the magnet is lowered into the water, its magnetic force lifts the screw.

A weak magnetic force can only pass through a thin layer of material. Strong magnetic forces can work across bigger gaps and through thicker materials.

The poles of a magnet

Magnetic force is strongest at the ends of a magnet. The ends are called the **poles.** Explore what happens when you put the poles of two magnets together.

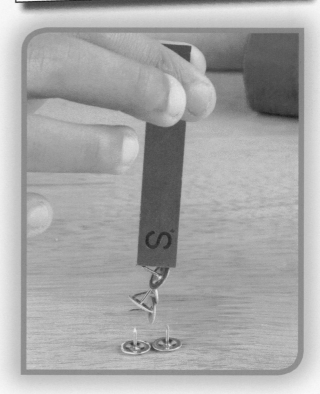

1 Bring one end of one magnet toward one end of the other. What happens?

Most thumbtacks stick to the ends or poles of the magnet.

18

2 Turn one of the magnets around and move the other end toward the first magnet. What happens now?

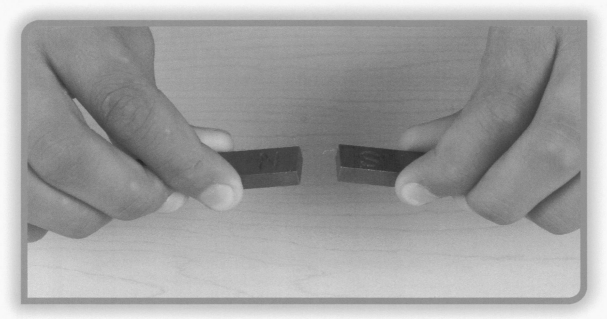

Do the ends pull together or push each other apart?

3 What happens when you turn both magnets around?

Check your results on page 28.

North and South Poles

Every magnet has a north **pole** and a south pole. When the north pole of one magnet is moved toward the south pole of another magnet, the magnets are pulled, or **attracted**, toward each other.

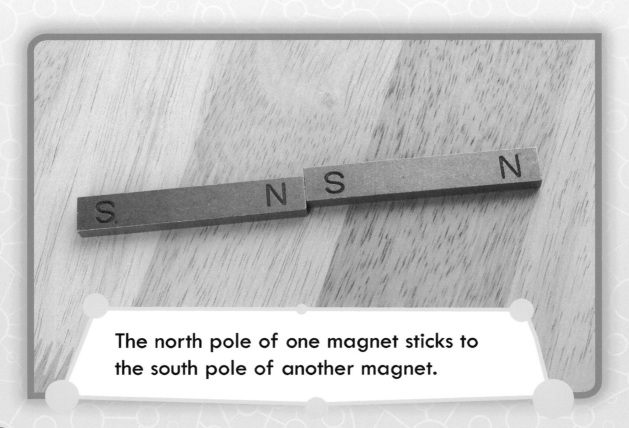

The north pole of one magnet sticks to the south pole of another magnet.

Can you make two like poles touch each other?

When you move two north poles or two south poles together, they push each other away. Like poles **repel** each other, but unlike poles attract.

Maglev Train

Maglev trains are extremely fast and have no wheels. They move so fast because they do not touch the track. Instead they lift up a short distance and "fly" through the air.

A Maglev train is driven by the force of magnetism.

A Maglev train floats just above the track.

A Maglev train has large magnets underneath it. The track includes electric coils, which become magnets when electricity flows through them. The coils **repel** the magnets under the train to lift it up.

Earth Is a Magnet

Earth is a giant magnet. The rocks around the center of Earth are made mostly of hot, liquid iron. The iron forms a huge magnet.

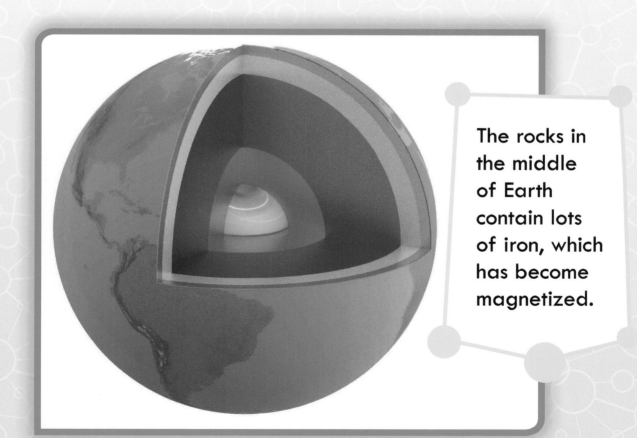

The rocks in the middle of Earth contain lots of iron, which has become magnetized.

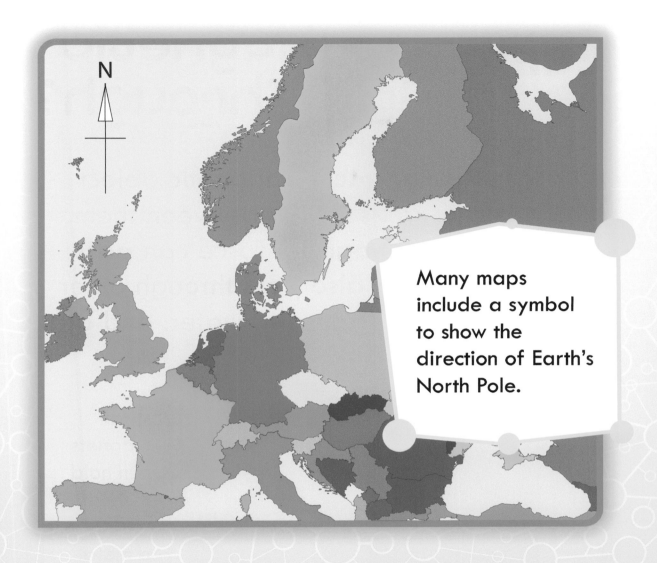

N

Many maps include a symbol to show the direction of Earth's North Pole.

Earth's magnet has two **poles,** one at each end. One points to the North Pole in the Arctic. The other pole points to the South Pole in Antarctica.

Using a Compass

A **compass** helps people to find their way. It has a magnet in the shape of a needle, which rotates around its center. When the needle comes to rest, it lines up with Earth's magnet and so points north.

The compass is turned until north on the compass lies at the end of the needle.

A hiker turns the map until the symbol for north points the same way as the compass needle.

Many people use information beamed from **satellites** to find their way. But aircraft pilots, ship crews, and many hikers still use a compass to keep them on course.

Experiment Results
What happened?

Magnetic or nonmagnetic (page 8)

Only objects made of certain metals, usually iron and steel, are magnetic. Most materials are not magnetic.

Which magnet is the strongest? (page 14)

The strongest magnet is the one whose magnetic force moves the nail from farthest away.

The poles of a magnet (page 18)

Whichever way you turn the magnets around, opposite **poles** will **attract** each other, and like poles will **repel** each other (see page 20).

Quiz

1 Aluminum and plastic are
  a both magnetic
  b both nonmagnetic
  c one is magnetic, but not the other

2 The magnet can attract the screw through water.
  a true
  b false

3 A **Maglev train** is driven by
  a magnetic force
  b electricity
  c diesel oil

Turn to page 31 for the answers.

Glossary

attract pull toward something

compass device that shows the direction of the North Pole

keeper iron bar placed against the ends of a magnet when it is not being used to help keep its magnetism

Maglev train train that is driven by magnetic force

pole end of a magnet where the magnetic force is strongest

recycling center place where materials are processed so that they can be used again

repel push something away

satellite object in space that travels around a much larger object, such as Earth

scrap metal things made of metal that have been thrown away

Find Out More

Books

Kenney, Karen Latchana. *Magnets* (Amicus Readers). Mankato, Minn.: Amicus, 2011.

Lawrence, Ellen. *Magnets* (Fun-Damental Experiments). New York: Bearport, 2015.

Parker, Steve. *Fizzing Physics* (Science Crackers). Mankato, Minn.: QEB, 2012.

Weakland, Mark. *Magnets Push, Magnets Pull* (A+ Books). Mankato, Minn.: Capstone, 2011.

Internet sites

Facthound offers a safe, fun way to find Internet sites related to this book. All of the sites on Facthound have been researched by our staff.

Here's all you do:
Visit www.facthound.com
Type in this code: 9781484626900

Index